AFTER THE BREAKUP: A SELF-LOVE JOURNAL

AFTER THE BREAKUP

A SELF-LOVE JOURNAL

Prompts and Practices to

Help You Get Over Your Ex

Lindsey Dortch Brock, LCSW

ROCKRIDGE
PRESS

Interior and Cover Designer: Monica Cheng
Art Producer: Janice Ackerman
Editor: Mo Mozuch
Production Editor: Nora Milman
Production Manager: Holly Haydash

Illustration: ©Anugraha Design/Creative Market
Author Photo: Courtesy of Ariel Shumaker Photography

Paperback ISBN: 978-1-63807-040-5
R0

This journal belongs to

_____

CONTENTS

Learning to Let Go

81

Replenishing Your Self-Worth

109

Getting Back Out There

137

INTRODUCTION

Chances are you're going through a pretty rough time right now. I imagine you'd really, *really* like for this part of your life to hurry up and pass, right?

I wish it worked that way. When I went through a breakup in my 20s, which my friends affectionately called "The Breakup of all breakups," that's exactly what I wanted—for life to pass by quickly so I could spend less time feeling alone, anxious, depressed, hurt, and confused.

I became a social butterfly and filled all my free time with friends or new dates. I poured myself into my work, leaving no time for feelings of sadness. I committed to giving an enthusiastic "Yes!" anytime I was offered an invitation to anything. (I somehow ended up in Little Rock, Arkansas, at a Taylor Swift concert. Can't say I regret it.) From the outside it looked like I was feeling happy and satisfied, unaffected by The Breakup. But the moments of quiet and stillness were unbearable for me. I woke up one day and realized that my life was being dictated by the avoidance of my awfully unpleasant internal experience.

That's where this journal comes in. I wish I had it all those years ago when I was hoping time would pass faster, because I didn't understand that the only way out of my anxiety and depression was to work through it.

The prompts in this journal are intended to help you slow down, if only for a few moments. In this slowdown, you will be able to reflect upon and record your unhelpful coping skills and untrue beliefs you have about yourself, your ex, and your relationships. Slowing down will help create space for you to connect to yourself and the grief you're experiencing. The sections within this journal will guide you through your breakup journey, providing prompts, stories, and musings every step of the way. Although grief isn't linear and there are no universal steps to mourn the end of a relationship, this journal is intended to be used from start to finish.

First, you'll begin by accepting the realities in front of you while bolstering your self-love and support from others. After the hardest days have passed and you've learned to be in a healthier relationship with your emotions, you'll begin to look at how you can let go of the relationship, move through the pain, accept your feelings, and ultimately find a new, healthier love when you're ready.

I promise it won't always feel this hard.

A NOTE ON VISUALIZATIONS

Guided imagery and visualizations can impact you in several ways; they can soothe the nervous system, help you relax, invite forgiveness, or increase your tolerance of uncomfortable feelings. When you come to a guided visualization exercise in this journal, keep these guidelines in mind:

▶ Quiet your surroundings to limit your distractions. These exercises are intended to create or connect to an internal emotional experience, and external sounds from beeping phones or loud housemates make it more difficult to tune inward.

▶ Get comfortable to better relax. Choose a place that feels safe and isn't charged with emotional memories. This may mean a favorite chair or laying on your bed. Just don't fall asleep!

▶ Stay present by noticing how your back feels against the chair and how your feet feel resting on the floor, for example. Some exercises prompt you to recall unpleasant emotions. For these exercises, staying aware of present-day sensations *while* accessing difficult emotions will help desensitize your body to and process these feelings.

▶ Take deep breaths from your diaphragm throughout the exercise. This will help you stay emotionally regulated and present.

▶ You can stop the exercise at any time if you feel unable to continue for whatever reason.

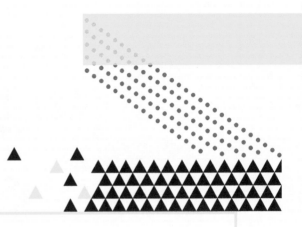

A Note on Safety

Although this journal leans heavily on themes, interventions, and exercises often used in my therapy office, it is not intended to replace therapy or professional support. If you are experiencing suicidal thoughts or feel at risk of harming yourself or others, please seek support through a local crisis center, emergency department, or via the National Suicide Prevention Lifeline (800-273-8255). If you are currently in a physically, emotionally, or sexually abusive relationship, please seek immediate support with a local therapist. There is a list of resources in the back of the book to help you explore your options.

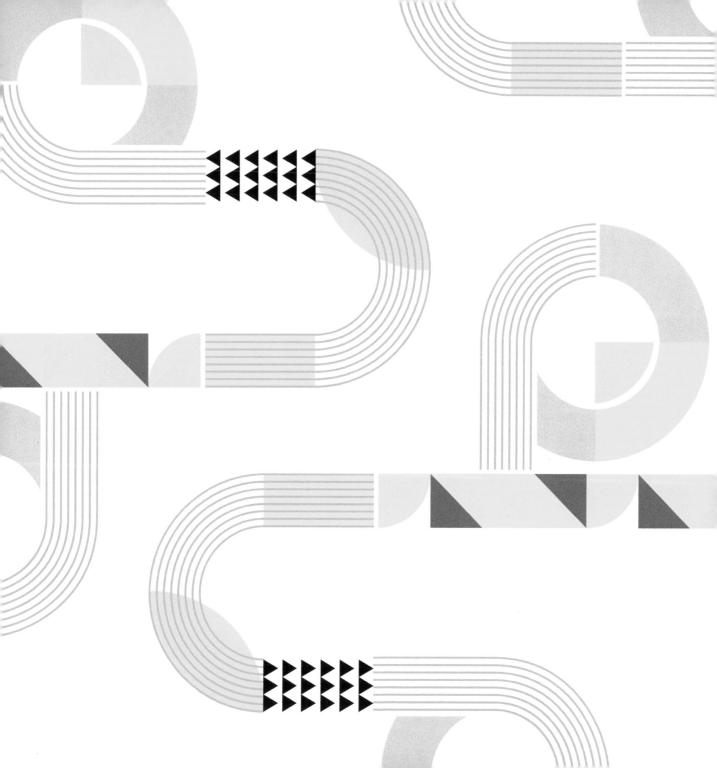

PROCESSING THE BREAKUP

The following prompts and stories will help you normalize the intense feelings you're experiencing while establishing a new way of relating to yourself and these emotions. Don't skip this section! You'll learn how to tolerate emotions instead of avoiding them as you begin to understand that your feelings don't need to change in order for you to be okay. Creating a new way to relate to your emotions is going to change your life, if you let it.

There's Gotta Be Something Wrong with Me

I thought I was going crazy. I couldn't stop checking my phone, looking at his social media, or walking by his apartment. I remember thinking, "Am I seriously walking by his place just to catch a glimpse of him? What is wrong with me?!"

There wasn't anything wrong with me. And there's nothing wrong with you, either. I was withdrawing from dopamine and oxytocin, the feel-good hormones that the brain releases when we experience intimacy, touch, and love. The reward center of my brain had been lighting up on the regular for a year and a half. My brain released dopamine and oxytocin when I would see his texts, enjoy his embrace, or laugh at his jokes. Then suddenly my main source of feel-good hormones was gone. Just like that.

Rationally, I knew his name was unlikely to show up on my phone. I knew that looking at his social media wasn't bringing us closer together. I knew walking by his place did not change our relationship status.

And yet I couldn't help myself. I didn't understand that my body was going through a literal withdrawal. And I certainly didn't realize that I was putting off my healing every time I looked at old pictures or asked a mutual friend how he was doing. The behaviors that had me feeling so crazy were driven by a hunt for dopamine and oxytocin. I just wanted to feel less terrible.

Driven by Withdrawal?

Consider your behaviors following the breakup. Make a list of four behaviors that might have been driven by a hunt for oxytocin and dopamine, but that you suspect weren't *actually* what was best for your healing. Then, go through your list and write down what feelings might have been driving each behavior or decision.

1. _____
   _____
   _____
   _____

2. _____
   _____
   _____
   _____

3. _____
   _____
   _____
   _____

4. _____
   _____
   _____
   _____

Thawing My Shock

Maybe you're surprised by the circumstances of the breakup or the intensity of the feelings you're experiencing. This shock is normal, so try not to judge yourself for feeling surprised, in denial, confused, etc.

Shock can make you freeze, leaving you feeling paralyzed and unable to move forward and process your grief.

▶ If you could thaw just a little bit, what feelings would you discover underneath the freeze?

▶ How are these feelings showing up in your body, your conversations, and your actions?

▶ What have been helpful ways to cope?

_____

_____

_____

_____

_____

_____

_____

_____

_____

_____

NAME IT TO TAME IT

Take a deep breath and tune in to your body. Circle any feelings you're noticing right now. You can't process your feelings if you don't know that they're there. Use this list as a reference whenever you need to better understand how you're feeling. You don't need to do anything about these feelings. Just notice them and allow them to exist.

- ○ Abandoned
- ○ Afraid
- ○ Ambivalent
- ○ Angry
- ○ Anxious
- ○ Ashamed
- ○ Bitter
- ○ Broken
- ○ Devalued
- ○ Disappointed
- ○ Disrespected
- ○ Embarrassed
- ○ Enraged
- ○ Fearful
- ○ Frustrated
- ○ Guilty
- ○ Hopeless
- ○ Hysterical
- ○ Insecure
- ○ Jealous
- ○ Lonely
- ○ Lost
- ○ Lovesick
- ○ Miserable
- ○ Remorseful
- ○ Resentful
- ○ Sad
- ○ Shattered
- ○ Terrified
- ○ Unloved
- ○ Unwanted
- ○ Used
- ○ Violated
- ○ Vulnerable
- ○ Weak
- ○ Worried

Treating Myself Differently This Time

Most people are a LOT harder on themselves than they are on their friends. It's much easier to judge yourself for having intense feelings, or to have unfair expectations of how you are coping with these emotions. What advice and support would you give a friend who is experiencing all that you're feeling during this breakup?

_____

_____

_____

_____

_____

_____

Now, be sure to treat yourself with this same compassion, understanding, and patience.

Something you must remember throughout this healing journey is that your feelings aren't permanent. Remembering this will change the trajectory of your healing (and life)!

The Magic in the Pause

Viktor Frankl, a neurologist, psychologist, and Holocaust survivor, famously said, "Between stimulus and response there is a space. In that space is our power to choose our response. In our response lies our growth and our freedom."

Without that pause, you are simply reacting to your emotions. I want to help you *respond* to your emotions instead of *react* to them. What do you know about this pause and how you relate to it? How can you cultivate more of it?

_____

_____

_____

_____

_____

_____

_____

_____

_____

_____

_____

_____

_____

_____

TENDING TO YOUR PHYSICAL HEALTH

After a breakup, it's important to focus on taking care of your physical health. Research conducted by psychologists from Ohio State University and the University of Arizona shows that a breakup affects the nervous and immune systems leading to sleep disturbances, appetite fluctuations, and even an increase in physical pain. MRIs have shown that the effects of a breakup on a person are similar to the effects of withdrawing from cocaine!

You may be experiencing withdrawal symptoms including appetite change, irritability, an increased need for sleep, and mood swings. Engaging in certain activities can replace the dopamine your brain's been missing, as well as endorphins to help ease the pain.

Lace up and get outside for a walk. Stretch your body throughout the day. Not only does it feel great, but it also helps your stuck emotions move through your body. Enjoy a delicious meal or an activity that used to bring you joy. Engaging in these types of activities can release endorphins, helping ease your sensations of both physical and emotional pain.

Making Space for the Uncomfortable

You know when a friend asks, "How are you doing?" and you reply, "Fine! Good! I'm good," and you both know it's a lie? A good friend will say, "No, how are you *really* doing?" Take a deep breath and ask yourself, "How am I *really* doing these days?" Be honest. Try to accept wherever you are in this process, even if it's hopeless, disappointing, or painful. Write about it here.

_____

_____

_____

_____

_____

_____

_____

_____

_____

_____

_____

_____

_____

_____

Practicing Compassion

It's important to be gentle, patient, and compassionate with yourself. Beating yourself up for feeling any type of way makes it near impossible to move through, process, or release emotions. Jot down your "go-to" self-talk that is too harsh. Then, brainstorm a new way to engage in self-talk that is filled with kindness or patience. How do you want to treat yourself? For example, when you notice self-loathing arise, what are some other ways you can respond to yourself in a more helpful, healthy way?

_____

_____

_____

_____

_____

_____

_____

_____

_____

_____

_____

_____

_____

_____

_____

CATCHING MY BREATH

Breathing is the foundation for all other bodily functions, yet you probably rarely give it the attention it deserves. Research shows that when you breathe with slow, controlled breaths, you can lower your blood pressure, calm your brain, improve your immune system, and regulate your emotions.

There are countless breathing exercises that may be helpful to explore. Four-square breathing, or box breathing, is a simple introduction to controlled breath:

1. Inhale through your nose for four slow seconds.

2. Hold your breath for four seconds.

3. Slowly release your breath through your mouth over four seconds.

4. Repeat until you notice a shift toward calm.

Today, set five alarms. These are reminders to breathe for two minutes. Sprinkle these reminders throughout your day for times you'll need to slow down, reset, and calm your nervous system. Can you give yourself just 10 minutes today? You're worth it, I promise.

You Can't Outrun It Forever

As a kid, Obie learned to avoid his feelings through exercise. This was his tried-and-true coping skill, and for a while, it really worked for him.

But the way young Obie learned to avoid feelings followed him into adulthood. Whenever he felt anxiety, insecurity, or fear, he would try to literally outrun it. Obie became a long-distance runner and would lace up anytime he needed to escape.

I started seeing Obie three months after his breakup. He had been "managing" his feelings with daily 15-mile runs. He ran so much that he injured himself and was unable to exercise. He didn't know any other way to deal with emotions, and it was torturing him to sit still and feel everything. He had never done it before.

Over time, Obie learned to recognize, name, and feel his emotions. As his tolerance for this discomfort grew, his relationship to running changed. He still laced up most days, but it was because he *wanted* to, not because he *needed* to in order to cope.

There is a whole different life out there for you that doesn't involve running from your emotions. I think you'll find it very freeing.

Getting to Know My Pain

What are the two most consuming or intense emotions you've been feeling since the breakup? Anger and sadness? Grief and loneliness? Where do they show up in your body?

_____

_____

_____

_____

_____

_____

Write down a plan for how you hope to respond to these emotions the next time you experience them. Remember, don't try to "fix" them or make them disappear.

_____

_____

_____

_____

_____

_____

_____

RECLAIMING MY DREAMS

Sleep is such an important part of healing. Your brain processes the events of your day during REM sleep, leaving you clearheaded and relaxed in the morning.

But after a breakup, your sleep is often one of the first things to be affected due to stress, anxiety, and heartbreak. Often, restlessness, racing thoughts, or even dreams of your ex will disrupt your sleep after a breakup.

Whatever your sleep disturbance, it's important to create a routine around bedtime. Limit your exposure to emotional triggers before bed (certain television shows or social media platforms). Create a relaxing environment for sleep through music, scents, or acts of self-care (like stretching, baths, or meditating). Studies show that the nervous system appreciates routine, as it creates predictability and a sense of control.

Do not expect immediate results from your new soothing evening routine. Commit to following this routine nightly for a week and notice any shifts in your sleep. Don't forget that your dreams often reflect the state in which you fell asleep. So, a more relaxed nervous system may yield fewer dreams about your ex!

Learning to Respond vs. React

Reflect on a time this week when you were experiencing intense emotions. How did you react to them? How would you like to respond to them next time? (*Example: "I was feeling anxious and hopeless. I called my ex three times and immediately regretted it. Next time I feel anxious and hopeless, I hope to call a friend or go for a walk."*)

_____

_____

_____

_____

_____

_____

_____

_____

_____

_____

_____

_____

_____

_____

Reflecting on the Past

Think about your family for a moment. What were the rules around intense feelings in your household growing up? Were you punished for big feelings or told to "toughen up"? Was everything swept under the rug? Write about your family history with feelings and big emotions here.

_____

_____

_____

_____

_____

_____

_____

_____

_____

_____

Have all of your emotions,
but don't let them have you.

Learning to Ride the Wave

I often use the analogy of riding a wave with my clients. Maybe you feel like you're on a surfboard and you can see the enormous wave approaching. You're terrified, so you start to frantically paddle away. Or maybe you've already been swept up in the wave and it's pushing you deeper and deeper toward the ocean floor.

Here, the wave represents the intense emotions you've been feeling. You can't tame a wave. Explore how you can *ride* the wave instead of being taken down by it. Hypothesize how to trust that a feeling can't hurt you, and to let the emotions *just exist* as you ride them out. What does it look like to practice that, instead of working so hard to escape them? (Buddhists call this "mindfulness.")

Noticing, Not Judging

What are your beliefs about the feelings you're experiencing now? That there is something wrong with you or that it'll never end? The grief and pain you are experiencing is entirely normal. It's not a problem, and there's nothing wrong (even though it sucks to feel this way!). When you start to pathologize your feelings, things get a little trickier. If you can familiarize yourself with these thoughts, you can catch them before you start to believe them. This "catch" can help prevent your grief from sliding into depression. Notice the thoughts and judgments you've had about your feelings. Write them down here.

_____

_____

_____

_____

_____

_____

_____

_____

_____

_____

_____

_____

Understanding the Intensity

When I went through a breakup, the intensity of my emotions didn't really make sense to me. While my feelings were valid, they also seemed much harder, deeper, and more intolerable than I expected them to be.

When the emotion feels disproportionate to the event, or it rationally "doesn't make sense" to be affected so much by it, that's an indicator of trauma. Your body is not only responding to the present-day trauma and loss, but it's also responding to all the other times you've felt this way before. Oftentimes, returning to the past helps you heal the present. Notice the intense feeling in your body. When have you felt this way before? Write about it here.

Confronting the Ways I Cope

Write down all of the ways you've coped since the breakup. This includes strategies you are proud of and the ones that make you cringe.

▶ When you're lonely, do you isolate, go out on the town, or something else?

▶ How do you cope at night versus during the day?

▶ How do you cope on a workday versus the weekend?

▶ Which strategies were helpful in the long term?

▶ Which outlets served more as a bandage and left you feeling worse afterward?

Recognize what was helpful and make a plan for the future so you can intentionally cope in ways that feel helpful.

_____

_____

_____

_____

_____

_____

_____

_____

_____

_____

NEW LOOK, NEW ENERGY

Have you gotten a haircut yet? Anecdotal reports from therapists and hairstylists alike suggest that this is a popular way to regain confidence, shed bad energy, and take back control after a breakup. For better or worse, your appearance is one of the few things you can control or manipulate. A haircut is a safe, low-risk way to exert control when you are reeling from the end of a relationship.

You don't need to get a haircut to change things up (but don't let me stop you). There are other ways to bring new energy into your life. Find comfort in rearranging the furniture, a simple wardrobe update, or bringing different lighting or incense into your spaces. These are all subtle, healthy ways to help you feel more confident, in control, and back on the path to yourself.

Celebrating What I've Accepted . . .

When you accept the hand that you've been dealt you can begin to heal. Acceptance doesn't mean you like the hand you're holding, or that you fold because "It is what it is, so what's the point?" It's a simple acknowledgment of "what is." What have you already accepted about this relationship and subsequent breakup as you've begun to heal?

_____

_____

_____

_____

_____

_____

_____

_____

_____

_____

_____

_____

_____

_____

_____

_____

. . . And Acknowledging There's More to Do

Without acceptance that this relationship is over, you cannot begin to heal. What has been difficult for you to accept about this relationship or the breakup? Why do you think it has been so hard to recognize these things as true? Resistance may indicate your need to take ownership of some of your past behaviors or your role in the end of the relationship.

_____

_____

_____

_____

_____

_____

_____

_____

_____

_____

_____

_____

_____

_____

_____

_____

Taking a Hard Look

It's time to consider the ways in which this relationship didn't serve you. Write about it here.

_____

_____

_____

_____

_____

_____

_____

_____

_____

_____

_____

_____

_____

_____

_____

_____

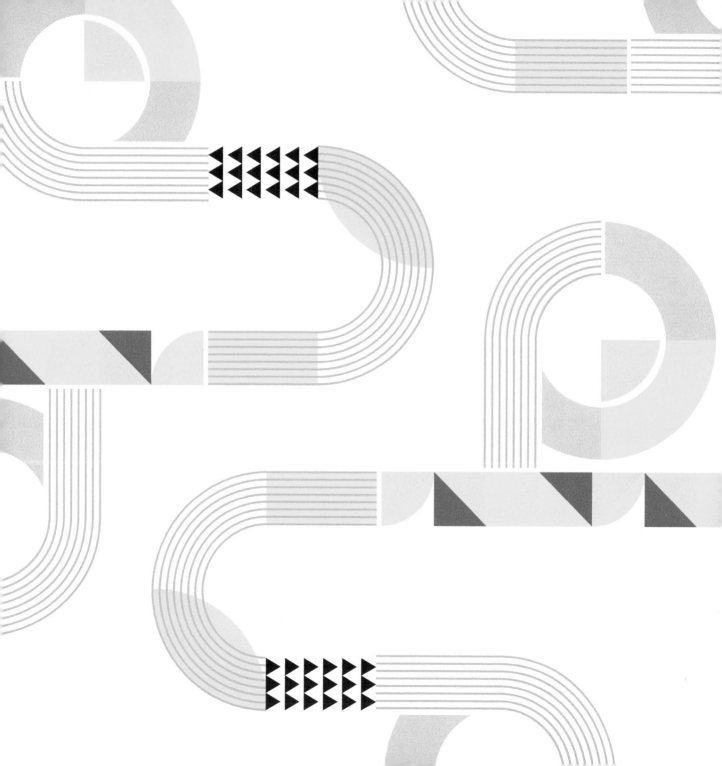

PUTTING YOURSELF FIRST

This section is all about putting yourself first. Your body is going through an intense emotional process as you learn to cope with this post-relationship new normal. If you experienced a *physical* injury, you'd expect to rest, recover, and rebuild. An emotional injury of this nature requires the same, and the following prompts are meant to encourage honesty about real self-care and help you confront self-destructive behaviors. Get ready to level with yourself about what you *need* in the long term, even if it's not what you *want* right now.

Give Yourself Some Credit!

Any chance you're doing better than you realized? I ask my clients to look for "weird measures of growth" to remind them that they're moving forward, healing, and surviving. Many people think that crying less, a decrease in anxiety, or readiness to date are the only markers of emotional growth and healing. In reality, there are many measures of growth that are often more subtle, discreet, or obscure.

Maybe at first, you can only see how awful you're doing. But look closer; you ate breakfast before thinking about your ex, or you noticed you weren't jealous when your best friend moved in with their partner. Write at least three examples of "doing better" that go beyond the societal expectations of "doing better." Nothing is too small. Add to this list throughout your healing journey to help you track your progress.

1. _____
   _____
   _____
   _____

2. _____
   _____
   _____
   _____

3. _____
   _____
   _____
   _____

AVOIDING YOUR FEELINGS DOESN'T MAKE THEM GO AWAY

There are as many unique ways to avoid feelings as there are humans in this world. While it's important to recognize when you're avoiding your feelings, it's equally necessary to make a plan to process them later. An entire internal experience is happening inside of you whether you acknowledge it or not! But it's impossible to heal unless you make space for your feelings and allow them to move through you. Try the following:

1. Limit any distractions so you may better connect to your inner emotional experience.

2. Set a timer for five minutes.

3. Close your eyes and notice what physical sensations you feel in your body. What do you feel when you think about your ex?

4. Become aware of these feelings and remind yourself you don't need to change them.

5. Expect your mind to wander. When you notice your attention has drifted away from your body to your thoughts, gently redirect your mind to the physical sensations in the body. Just allow the thoughts to exist.

This exercise teaches you to exist with your emotions rather than trying to change them. When you can simply exist with these feelings, you'll be able to process and move through them. Notice how you feel after giving yourself space to feel it all.

You've Probably Done This
(If You're Anything Like Me)

What are the rationalizations you've given yourself for talking to your ex or answering their texts? Write them all down below. If you can name them now, it's easier to challenge them later, making it more likely you'll respond in a way that nurtures your healing (such as not responding to them at all!).

_____

_____

_____

_____

_____

_____

_____

_____

_____

_____

_____

_____

_____

_____

_____

Have I Felt This Way Before?

How did your ex hurt you in ways that you've been hurt before? Get to know the history of this hurt so you may extend more compassion to yourself. Understanding the depth of this pain will help you be less judgmental toward yourself and can point to other losses you need to grieve.

_____

_____

_____

_____

_____

_____

_____

_____

_____

_____

_____

_____

_____

_____

Deserving of More Than a Band-Aid

Today, notice how you feel when you (inadvertently) remind your brain of your ex. This may look like browsing through old pictures, reading notes or texts from them, viewing or engaging with their social media, or driving by old stomping grounds.

You will likely feel a smidge better, for a nanosecond. But notice how you feel *after* that nanosecond. Reflect on those feelings here.

_____

_____

_____

_____

_____

_____

_____

_____

_____

_____

_____

_____

_____

_____

Befriending Boundaries

A boundary is something you're willing or unwilling to tolerate. A boundary is for yourself, not a rule you make for someone else to follow.

Example: "I don't want to talk to my ex. So, if my ex reaches out to me, I won't respond. I will respect and hold my own boundary." This is different from *"I need to get my ex to stop texting me, because that's my boundary! And if they cross that boundary, I'll text them to rant about it."* The boundary is all about *how* you *want to respond* and *what behaviors* you *are and are not willing to tolerate.*

What boundaries do you need to have for yourself as you navigate this breakup?

_____

_____

_____

_____

_____

_____

_____

Walking away from someone you love may be the hardest thing you'll ever have to do.

YOU CAN DO LITERALLY ANYTHING ELSE

Make a list of 12 things you could do instead of texting your ex, answering their call, or reaching out in any way. Reference this list when the urge to reach out to them is very strong and it feels hard to hold your boundary. I know you can go no contact!

1. _____
2. _____
3. _____
4. _____
5. _____
6. _____
7. _____
8. _____
9. _____
10. _____
11. _____
12. _____

Wait, Self-Care Is More Than a Bubble Bath?

What does self-care mean to you? Is it easy to practice self-care, or does it seem like a waste of time? Notice any resistance to taking time for yourself and write about it here.

_____

_____

_____

_____

_____

_____

_____

_____

_____

_____

_____

_____

_____

_____

_____

_____

_____

_____

Using (or Creating) Your Deep Bench

After Monique broke up with her girlfriend, she relied heavily on her best friend Jackie for several weeks. She felt so lucky to have Jackie there to lift her up when she started feeling overwhelmed by her complicated grief.

Monique lived with Jackie the first week post breakup. Jackie welcomed Monique, so Monique gladly accepted the offer to crash in the guest room. Jackie stayed up late with her as she processed the betrayal and grief Monique was experiencing. She made meals for her friend, made sure Monique got out of bed for work, and supported her friend the best way she knew how.

At the start of week two, Jackie mentioned that it would probably be best for Monique to go back to her own place and sleep there. Monique feared she had done something wrong and was worried Jackie was upset. Monique went back home to sleep, but came to Jackie's house after work for dinner every night. It was too much to think about being by herself.

By the third week of Monique's daily visits, Jackie wasn't around as much. She began working late and telling Monique she was unavailable. Monique was confused and not sure what to make of this. It felt like her best friend was breaking up with her, too.

It's perfectly normal and healthy to lean on friends for support. However, when you are experiencing the trauma of a breakup, it's really easy to forget that other people are experiencing the stresses and demands of life, too.

Check in with your friends before you start to lean on them too heavily. Don't make assumptions about their capacity to support you indefinitely. Ask them to share about their lives, too, as you navigate this life-altering moment in time. A therapist once told me, "Be sure to spread your needs around so they don't pile up in one place or with one person. Always, for anything, spread your needs around."

Show Yourself Some Love!

Write a love letter to yourself. What makes you amazing? Why are folks glad to know you? Don't be shy! It's really important to remember there's a really amazing person in there, even if you can't see it right now.

_____

_____

_____

_____

_____

_____

_____

_____

_____

_____

_____

_____

_____

_____

_____

_____

_____

NAMING MY NEEDS AND ASKING FOR SUPPORT

Ask yourself, "What do I need right now from a friend or support person?" You may need to vent about your ex, space to be mad, a moment to dream about the future, or to be a listening ear to someone else. Decide what you need at this moment in your journey and pick up the phone to go after it.

Your Needs Can Change, So Keep Up!

At different times in your healing, you may need different things, and there is no "right" way to practice self-care. When you have a deadline or a job to do, you may need to compartmentalize big-time. You just need to be *aware* of the coping mechanism you are using at any given time. What are the signs that you need a break? Brainstorm helpful ways to put space between you and your emotional intensity when you notice these signs.

_____

_____

_____

_____

_____

_____

_____

_____

"I think it's important to realize you can miss
something, but not want it back."

—PAULO COELHO

Understanding My Emotional Bubble Baths

Beyond pedicures and bath soaks (don't get me wrong, those are great, too!), what can you do to take care of your body and mind? Are there boundaries you need to set with friends and family, certain conversations you need to have or avoid right now, etc.? What does taking care of yourself really look like for you at this time?

_____

_____

_____

_____

_____

_____

_____

_____

_____

_____

_____

_____

_____

_____

_____

_____

Don't Believe Everything You Think

Notice the thoughts you are having about yourself as you cut ties with your ex. What (likely unhelpful or untrue) assumptions are you making about your ex as they, too, navigate no contact? Write them down below. Challenge them. Ask yourself if it's helpful to your healing for you to think this way.

_____

_____

_____

_____

_____

_____

_____

_____

_____

_____

_____

_____

_____

_____

Scheduling a Date . . . to Worry

Don't have time to worry or feel about it today? Make a note of whatever is coming up for you below. It'll keep. Come back to it later today or tomorrow when you have the time to process or feel what you're noticing. It's okay to put your feelings on a shelf for a minute, but it's really important to take them back down and unpack them at a later time.

_____

_____

_____

_____

_____

_____

Now that you have the time, energy, or capacity to explore the feelings or worries you've written about, notice how they feel *now*. What does it feels like to visit them at a later time? What can you learn through this exercise? Write about it here. Repeat this exercise as needed throughout your grief process.

_____

_____

_____

_____

_____

Understanding My Triggers

It's time to get to know your triggers.

▶ What makes your anxiety spike?

▶ What topics, people, or places make the tears come?

▶ Which thoughts, people, or memories make you so angry that you can't function?

_____

_____

_____

_____

_____

_____

_____

_____

_____

_____

_____

_____

_____

_____

An Emotional Roadmap for Triggers

When you become more aware of your triggers, it's harder for them to catch you off guard. Sometimes you can plan to avoid your triggers when you recognize you're feeling unstable or unsure about your ability to manage them. Other times, you can know your triggers, confront them, and not be swayed by the emotions that come with them. That's what you're working toward, and it's okay if you're not there yet.

Rate the triggers you listed in the previous exercise (see page 43), from least to most intense. Write how you want to approach or engage with each of these triggers.

_____

_____

_____

_____

_____

_____

_____

_____

_____

_____

_____

_____

_____

_____

TAKE A BREAK TO SHOW SOME LOVE (TO OTHERS!)

At this point, you've spent a lot of time processing your own feelings and grief. Hopefully you've allowed yourself to lean on those who are close to you and have let them support you in your healing process. Give yourself a break from your intense emotional processing by holding space for someone else today. Your nervous system will thank you for taking a break from constant emoting, and it can feel really healthy to emotionally support your friends and family.

Out with the "Bad"

Let's shift out of the mindset of whether a coping mechanism is good or bad, right or wrong. Instead, when considering how to practice self-care, ask yourself if something is helpful or unhelpful to your healing. This language removes judgment from your behaviors while getting real about what is actually helpful to your healing.

For example, if you want to go to a concert tonight, that's not inherently good or bad. If you go because it feels like a great way to relax and connect with friends, go for it! That sounds really helpful! If you are going because you are hoping to catch a glimpse of your ex at the show, you should ask yourself whether that's helpful to your healing.

Reflect on shifting "good or bad" judgments to "helpful or unhelpful" and get real about times you've engaged in unhelpful coping mechanisms.

_____

_____

_____

_____

_____

_____

_____

_____

_____

_____

_____

Dragging Him Wasn't Helping Her

Andie was mad. She was coming to terms with the fact that her ex-partner lied to her daily for four years, cheated on her, and left no space for her in the relationship. Andie *definitely* had the right to be mad and she knew it, too. This anger was with her in every conversation and every interaction.

Although she had the right to this anger, the beliefs that came with it were keeping her in a victim mindset. She found herself telling anyone who would listen, "Can you believe my ex?" and "They are the worst thing that ever happened to me." In the moment, it felt good to have validation from her friends that, yes, in fact her ex *was* awful. But she began to notice she wasn't getting any better. She wasn't moving on after the breakup.

While Andie *was* a victim in some aspects of the relationship, her continued focus on her victimization allowed her ex to control her narrative and healing. When Andie started focusing on her own feelings and behaviors, she noticed a positive shift in her outlook and mood. Her conversations changed from talking about her ex to talking about herself. She acknowledged that she made excuses for the abuse, which allowed her to stay in the relationship. She began to recognize that she hadn't respected herself any more than her ex had.

I invite you to shift your focus from your ex's behaviors to your own behaviors. After all, that's the only thing you can control.

Reorienting My Narrative to Support Healing

Real talk: Do you have a victim mindset? Do you consider the breakup something that "happened to you"? If so, it's time to shift toward a more empowered mindset. How has thinking this way served you thus far? How is it holding you back from healing? Write about it here.

_____

_____

_____

_____

_____

_____

_____

_____

_____

_____

_____

_____

_____

_____

_____

_____

_____

CLEANING HOUSE

A "trigger" is an external stimulus that stirs up intense or overwhelming emotion. It's time to reduce the triggers in your home as you begin to navigate going no contact with your ex. (If you have yet to go "no contact," now is the time to stick to it.) So, grab a shoebox and begin to put some things away. Those pictures, letters, and keepsakes from your ex aren't helping you heal right now. In fact, they're working against your healing process because they keep you in your grief. There is no pressure or expectation to get rid of these items, but you'll benefit by keeping them out of sight.

Getting Cozy with "I Just Don't Know"

You may experience an increase in worry after you cut ties with your ex. You may worry about what they're doing, how they are coping, if they are seeing someone else, or whether they miss you. But worrying allows you to avoid the hard truth that you have *no idea* what your ex is doing or how they're feeling. That unknown can be *intolerable*. So instead, you worry.

▶ What are you worrying about?

▶ How is worrying serving you?

▶ What are some ways that you can tolerate truly not knowing what your ex is up to?

_____

_____

_____

_____

_____

_____

_____

_____

_____

_____

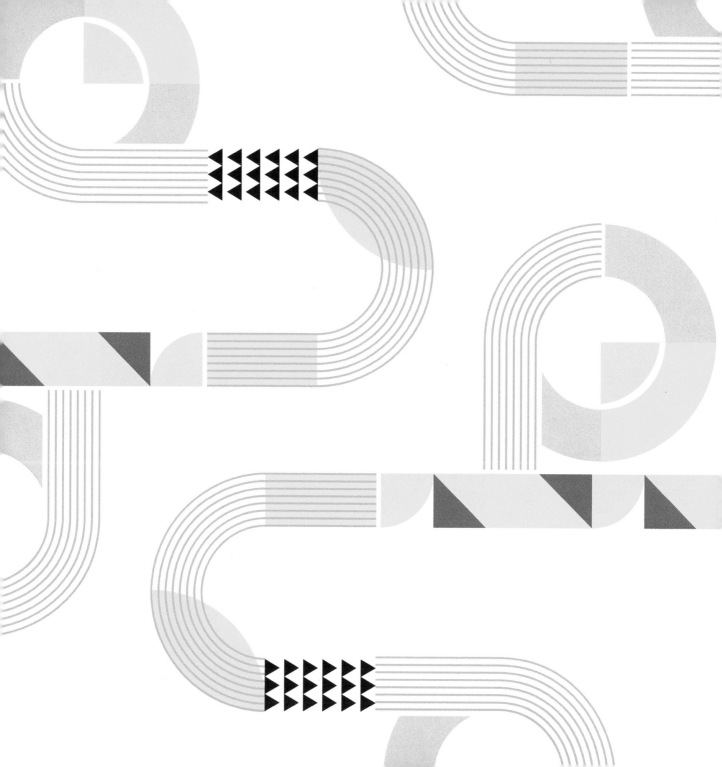

LEARNING FROM YOUR RELATIONSHIP

Hopefully, the last section helped you feel more confident in your ability to navigate the intense emotions of this breakup. With your new coping skills and boundaries in tow, it is time to confront your past relationships, your patterns, and yourself. The following prompts will help you unpack what went awry in your relationship. They'll guide you to hard truths and will help you take accountability for your role in this breakup, where appropriate. By increasing your awareness around your thought patterns, behaviors, and past relationships, you'll be better equipped to make different decisions next time.

What Does My Childhood Have to Do with My Partner?

Cora was always drawn to partners who seemed uninterested in her. She described the pattern: always chasing someone, never getting anywhere, and eventually running out of steam. This cycle allowed Cora to believe she was unworthy and undeserving of love. When she began therapy, her goal was to "learn to pick available partners."

Cora wasn't exaggerating. She described countless relationships that had a failure to launch. She realized she was repulsed by partners who outwardly gave her attention, affection, and time. Instead of judging herself for this repulsion, she decided to get curious about it. That's when Cora told me about her late father.

She described a loving, happy relationship with him and remembers him with high regard. I also learned he lived with extreme depression and intense anxiety, often escaping to the basement for weeks or months at a time. Although the good times were great, Cora had many unmet emotional needs. Cora was always chasing her dad for love, attention, and affection. More often than not, he wasn't able to outwardly reciprocate.

Cora began to understand she was trying to heal from unmet childhood needs through pursuing unavailable partners. Maybe, *just maybe*, if the unavailable men would change for *her,* then it would prove she was worthy of love.

As your awareness about your patterns increases, consider how past relationships are influencing present ones. Through her healing, Cora learned her worthiness of love is innate and didn't need others to prove it. Eventually, she was drawn to emotionally available men.

Do I Actually Want Personal Change?

Do you feel highly motivated to do *your* personal work (versus pinning it on your ex)? Maybe you're feeling hopeless and unmotivated to dig deep or look at hard things from your past. Without judgment, explore your motivation for change. It's important to be honest about where you are, and to go from there.

What do you hope will come with personal growth and change? Write about it here.

_____

_____

_____

_____

_____

_____

_____

_____

_____

_____

_____

_____

_____

_____

_____

Meandering through My Relationship Graveyard

What is your romantic relationship history? Writing it down here may help you notice any patterns. When you're more aware of your patterns, you can be more intentional with your choices in the future. Go back to the beginning. No relationship is too small or insignificant. Consider, too, the relationships that *didn't* happen, or that *almost* happened. Understanding these "almost relationships" as a part of your dating history can be helpful, too. Just notice what you notice!

_____

_____

_____

_____

_____

_____

_____

_____

_____

_____

_____

_____

_____

_____

_____

_____

I Don't Have a Type . . . Do I?

Explore any similarities your past partners or romantic interests have shared. Maybe they share personality traits, the breakups were under similar circumstances, or they all had a terrible sense of humor.

Get curious about the similarities. Does it seem like you have "a type"? Reflect on that here.

_____

_____

_____

_____

_____

_____

_____

_____

_____

_____

_____

_____

_____

_____

Examining My Role

Now that you've identified any similarities your past partners share, I invite you to explore *your* role in these relationships. Are you "The Fixer"? Or maybe "The Helper"? Did you lead or follow in relationships? How did you step into this role during childhood? Understanding the childhood origins of your patterns can help you step out of them in adulthood.

_____

_____

_____

_____

_____

_____

_____

_____

_____

_____

_____

_____

_____

_____

GETTING UNTANGLED FROM YOUR TRICKY THOUGHTS

The therapy modality cognitive behavioral therapy (CBT) is rooted in the belief that thoughts can affect emotions, and emotions can affect behaviors. If your thoughts can ultimately affect your behaviors, then you better make sure your thoughts are true, honest, and helpful.

In his book The Feeling Good Handbook, *Dr. David Burns popularized the concept of cognitive distortions by giving names to common manifestations of tricky, unhelpful, or untrue ways of thinking (a quick Google search for "list of cognitive distortions" will lead you to these common thought patterns). Familiarize yourself with this list so you can quickly recognize when you're engaging in unhelpful thinking patterns. Save it on your phone. Commit to reviewing this list twice daily for the next week.*

○ As you read the list of thought distortions, which ones felt familiar? Did any of them make you vigorously nod your head as if to say, "Oh yeah, that's me"?

○ Write down any untrue thoughts or beliefs you hold about your past relationship in the first column of the following table.

○ Replace these distortions with more reality-based thoughts in the second column. Reference this page as often as you need. Bring awareness to these patterns and work to rewrite the narrative to be fair, true, and reality based.

DISTORTION	TRUTHFUL REALITY
"If I were a better partner, they would have been happier and stayed."	*"There were many factors that led to the end."*

"Reality is a projection of your thoughts or the things you habitually think about."

—STEPHEN RICHARDS

When You Don't Even Recognize Yourself Anymore

People often talk of "losing parts of themselves" in a relationship. Sometimes this looks like not using your voice, tolerating bullshit, or neglecting your friends. Maybe it's as simple as never eating at your favorite restaurant, or forgoing baseball games during your relationship because your partner wasn't into it. What did you give up in order to be with your ex-partner? What would have happened if you hadn't given up those aspects of yourself? For each thing you gave up, note the reaction you think your partner would have had if you had held onto this part of you.

_____

_____

_____

_____

_____

_____

_____

_____

_____

_____

_____

_____

Not All Love Is Created Equally

Think about how your ex treated you and the type of love they gave you. Maybe they were doting, caring, and passive. Perhaps they were abusive and manipulative. Maybe they allowed room for fierce independence or felt really attached to you at all times.

Many people are attracted to partners that love in a familiar way. Write about how this love looks and feels to you, and explore when, and from whom, you first learned that this was love.

_____

_____

_____

_____

_____

_____

_____

_____

_____

_____

_____

_____

_____

_____

_____

_____

TEACHING YOURSELF HOW TO HAVE "JUST MEMORIES"

Like a stranger observing you and your ex, try to adopt a neutral perspective on your past relationship. Check any emotion at the door and simply reflect on the time together.

○ Reflect on your favorite memory of your ex.

○ Reflect on the most emotionally intense memory of your ex. The one that keeps you up at night or that you keep replaying in your head. This may be a pleasant or disturbing memory.

○ Call a trusted friend and practice sharing these memories as if you were a fly on the wall watching the relationship unfold, unaffected by the emotion captured in these memories. This practice helps you become less reactive to your memories. Practice making them "just memories."

Example of neutral memory recall: "We went to the Biltmore House together one day in June." Example of emotionally charged memory recall: "I surprised my ex with tickets to Biltmore, and it was so wonderful. They were so surprised. I'll never forget how romantic that day was or the look on their face when I handed them those tickets. It was the best day."

Well, Since You Asked . . .

What do you need to own about your role in the breakup? For example, did you allow certain behaviors you wish you had stood up to? Were you quick to anger or shift blame? Without any self-judgment, identify three behaviors or characteristics you need to recognize in yourself in order to take accountability.

1. _____

_____

_____

_____

2. _____

_____

_____

_____

3. _____

_____

_____

_____

When Pearls Are More than a Fashion Statement

As I flipped through old photos of my younger self, I saw one of me smiling at a football game with a boyfriend. Even now, I can remember under that smile I was feeling sad and frustrated with myself for skipping my best friend's birthday dinner. "I have these tickets; I'm sorry I can't make it," I told her. As much as I wanted to be with her, I felt obligated to go to the football game. My partner had purchased tickets for us, even though I had expressed that I didn't want to go.

Another picture catches my eye. Who was that girl wearing pearls? Do I even own any pearls now? A seemingly insignificant piece of jewelry represents much more to me: A desire to be accepted by others. A hope to form friendships. A fear that if I showed up without makeup or jewelry, I'd be too different. Out of a fear that it wasn't okay to be different, I wore the pearls.

There are dozens of other pictures that capture similar moments. For years, I ignored my true self in hopes of fitting in or making others happy. As I thumb through the pictures, I feel a sadness for my younger self. I also have compassion for her because she did the best she knew how to do at that time. But I'm never going back.

Being Honest with Yourself about Not Being Honest with Yourself

In your own words, define the term *self-betrayal*. Write about what that concept means to you and name three times you've engaged in small (or big!) acts of self-betrayal throughout your lifetime. For each example, write down what you were hoping to gain by betraying yourself. (Don't skip that last part!)

1. _____

_____

_____

_____

_____

2. _____

_____

_____

_____

_____

3. _____

_____

_____

_____

_____

WHAT DOES IT FEEL LIKE TO NOT TAKE CARE OF ME?

Read over your reflections on self-betrayal. Notice what you feel in your body as you acknowledge ways you didn't take care of yourself in the past. What do you feel? There are no expectations or "right or wrong ways to feel" right now. Just notice. Then, write those sensations here (Example: nausea in my abdomen, etc.).

_____

_____

Make a list of five things you want to extend to yourself when you recognize the feelings you wrote about in your body (Examples: acceptance, forgiveness, grace, patience, love). Invite these things to exist in you when you notice these feelings coming up in the future.

Example: When I notice the tightness in my chest, I will invite forgiveness and understanding to help me process my self-betrayal.

1. _____

_____

_____

_____

2. _____

_____

_____

_____

3. _____

_____

_____

_____

4. _____

_____

_____

_____

5. _____

_____

_____

_____

Reconciling the Good with the Bad

It's important to consider the relationship as a whole, remembering the good times with the bad. Only then can you begin to grieve the whole relationship.

What was good about your relationship? What characteristics, tendencies, or behaviors do you miss? Write about it here in a neutral, factual way.

_____

_____

_____

_____

_____

_____

_____

_____

_____

_____

_____

_____

_____

_____

_____

A PRACTICE IN HOLDING
FONDNESS WITH SADNESS

I invite you to try the following:

1. Close your journal and your eyes and follow your imagination.

2. Picture the living space where you and your ex spent most of your time together creating memories.

3. Notice where your brain and memories take you, and don't judge yourself for anything that pops into your head.

4. Begin mentally walking through the familiar living space. What memories are associated with different rooms?

5. Notice what physical sensations come up in your body as your mind walks you through the house/building/space/etc.

6. As the memories pop up, remind yourself that nothing is wrong if you are feeling sad, overwhelmed, angry, or anxious. Similarly, it's okay to have happy, exciting, or joyous memories, too.

7. Try to allow the feelings to just exist in your body. Don't rush to fix them or change them. Remind yourself that happy memories can exist among sad or hurtful memories. They don't negate each other. Practice letting them coexist.

Those Times I Didn't Pay Attention

When was the relationship really over? Even if the breakup surprised you or you initiated the end, challenge yourself to really wrestle with this question. Identify three times when you rejected or ignored that "knowing" voice inside of you that questioned your satisfaction in the relationship.

1. _____
   _____
   _____
   _____
   _____

2. _____
   _____
   _____
   _____
   _____

3. _____
   _____
   _____
   _____
   _____

Be honest with yourself about why you ignored what you knew and write about it here.

_____

_____

_____

_____

_____

_____

_____

_____

"Do not be embarrassed by your mistakes. Nothing can teach us better than our understanding of them. This is one of the best ways of self-education."

—THOMAS CARLYLE

Who Am I When I'm in a Relationship?

Many times, people let romantic relationships steal their focus, leaving friends or family members in the cold. Consider how you related to others while you were in a relationship with your ex. Celebrate how you were there for others and recognize where there's room for improvement. Use what you've learned about yourself from this past relationship to name characteristics and behaviors you'd like to carry with you as you move forward.

Keep Noticing

What have you noticed this week about any unhelpful ways of thinking? Write down any triggers that may lead to a thought spiral.

Example: "When I feel sad, I always think 'I will never get over this,'" or, "Every Friday I feel anxious because I assume my ex is having fun without me." The triggers here are sadness and Fridays.

It's harder to be caught off guard by your triggers when you can see them coming from a mile away. Write down at least five triggers and the unhelpful thoughts and behaviors that follow.

1. _____

_____

_____

_____

_____

_____

_____

2. _____

_____

_____

_____

_____

_____

3. _____

_____

_____

_____

_____

_____

_____

4. _____

_____

_____

_____

_____

_____

_____

5. _____

_____

_____

_____

_____

_____

_____

IT IS TIME FOR AN EX-LESS PARTY

It's time to celebrate! Make plans with a friend to celebrate your growth thus far. Look how far you've come! You've confronted your own patterns that led to the end of this relationship and have begun to hold yourself accountable for your past actions and future healing. As you celebrate, there's only one topic that's off-limits: your ex. Share this rule with your friend so they can help keep the focus on you as you celebrate your growth.

Looking at Loss with a Bird's-Eye View

Do you remember making timelines in elementary school? About the birth of a nation, the history of ice cream, or an outline of your life? Understanding the big picture helps integrate the past with the present.

Chart a timeline of the losses you've experienced in your life. Think broadly about loss: loss of jobs, friendships, pets, etc. Seeing the big picture will help you understand their interconnectedness and help you process your current loss. Chart the timeline and write your observations here.

_____

_____

_____

_____

_____

_____

_____

_____

_____

_____

_____

_____

_____

_____

So What Are We Missing?

This was a tough section. I asked you to confront parts of yourself that you likely would have preferred not to look at. I asked you to confront decisions you made that went against your best interests. So my question now is: What did you leave out?

   After reading certain prompts, did memories pop into your head that you chose not to write about? Did you ever decide to "look at that later" at any point in this section? Now is the time to acknowledge anything you've been avoiding within yourself. It will be worth it.

_____

_____

_____

_____

_____

_____

_____

_____

_____

_____

_____

_____

_____

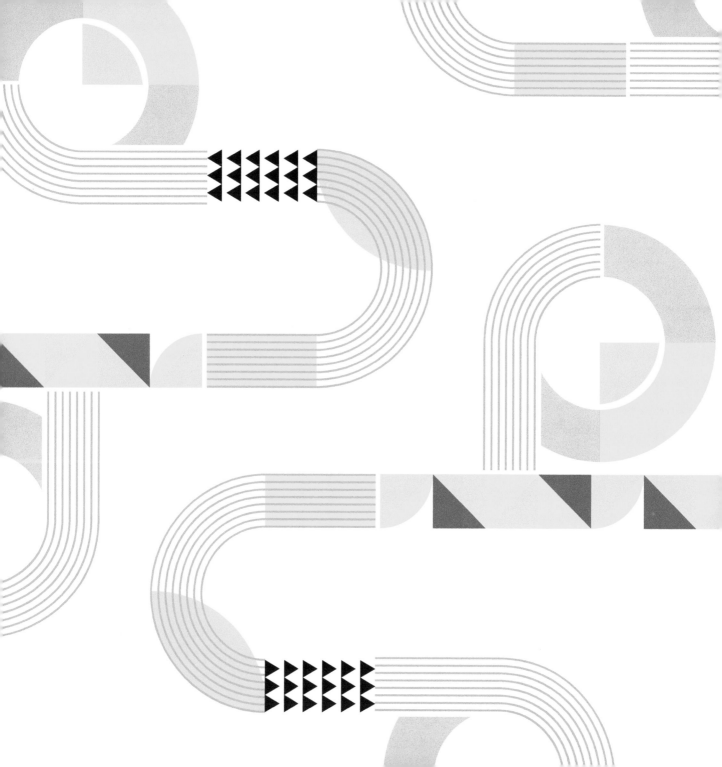

LEARNING TO LET GO

By now, you've confronted what this relationship was—and what it wasn't. Armed with a more honest understanding and acceptance of the way things were, you're ready to engage in the next layer of your healing. This section will support you in releasing anger and letting go of control as you learn to make peace with the way things are. You'll also learn how to better connect to your truest self. And when you can learn to do that, everything else becomes a little easier.

Understanding My Relationship with Control

What does "being in control" mean to you? How do you feel when you have control over a situation versus when you don't have it? Write about the role control plays in your life.

_____

_____

_____

_____

_____

_____

_____

_____

_____

_____

_____

_____

_____

_____

_____

_____

_____

Getting to Know My Anger

Try to recall your earliest memory that involved anger. Was it your anger or someone else's? What sensations do you notice in your body when you think about this memory? Write about the memory here and name two sensations you feel in your body as you recall that story.

_____

_____

_____

_____

_____

_____

_____

Expecting your ex to provide you with "closure" or believing that your healing depends on it is a myth. That's just not how it happens. The good news is that you can create this closure on your own.

When Anger Is a Front

Maybe you've heard the sentiment that "anger is a secondary emotion." This suggests that you feel outward anger to cover up a more vulnerable, scary, or intense primary feeling (for example, to avoid the internal sadness you feel, you may quickly move to outward anger). There are many cases where anger presents as secondary. Sometimes, though, anger is just anger!

How is anger manifesting in your breakup journey? Does your anger feel primary, secondary, or both? Understanding our anger helps us release it.

_____

_____

_____

_____

_____

_____

_____

_____

_____

_____

_____

_____

_____

_____

TAKING THE EDGE OFF YOUR INTENSE EMOTIONS

It can feel impossible to tolerate your anger when it feels intense, confusing, or all-consuming. When you pair bilateral stimulation with these feelings and sensations in the body, the intensity of these emotions decreases as you self soothe.

Bilateral stimulation is a method used in Eye Movement Desensitization and Reprocessing therapy (EMDR) that involves alternately tapping the right and left sides of your body. When you engage in bilateral stimulation, your whole brain begins to work together. Sometimes intense emotions or traumatic memories can encourage your brain to operate from a place of survival. Bilateral stimulation helps the brain operate in a more helpful way by prompting it to move from a state of survival to one of healing.

1. Cross your wrists across your chest and interlock your thumbs to create a "butterfly."

2. Connect to the sensations of anger in your body.

3. With your hands pointing upward toward your neck, slowly and gently tap your chest with alternating hands.

4. Notice the sensations and thoughts in your body. Don't try to change them; rather, observe them as they are happening.

5. Do this for five minutes if your tolerance allows.

6. Don't be surprised if you notice a decrease in emotional intensity.

I Didn't Know You Were a Fortune Teller

What assumptions do you have about your dating future? What are the story lines you believe about your lovability or worth? Remember, you have *no idea* what your future holds. None! Rewrite your narrative to become a more honest reflection. Practice tolerating uncertainty, and remember: These are just thoughts. They don't get to control you.

Example: "No one wants to date me. I am broken." In reality, I don't know what the future holds. I do know that many people have loved me in my lifetime. I know I can take things a day at a time as the future unfolds.

_____

_____

_____

_____

_____

_____

_____

_____

_____

_____

_____

_____

_____

Staying Curious about Forgiveness

Do you easily find your way to forgiveness? Or is it more difficult? In your relationship, were there things you found unforgivable? What *were* you able to forgive?

It's True, Whether I Like It or Not

"I have no control over how my ex feels about me, how they spend their time, or their judgments of me." Regardless of how you feel about it, this is a true statement.

Notice how that statement makes you feel as you read it again. Some people find this statement liberating. Most find it triggers anxiety. Reflect here and consider how you might make a mental shift to embrace this truth.

_____

_____

_____

_____

_____

_____

_____

_____

_____

_____

_____

_____

_____

_____

_____

_____

A MINDFUL PRACTICE IN LETTING GO

You will only let go of the past when you're ready to do so, and not a moment sooner. This exercise will help you identify what you are and aren't ready to release. It will help jump-start the process of letting go for when you are ready.

1. Imagine that you are standing on top of a mountain.

2. Picture in your mind the clear blue sky. Imagine the smells of grass, trees, and fresh water. Listen for birds chirping and try to feel the light breeze. You are relaxed.

3. In your hands is a bunch of balloons. Each balloon represents something you're leaving behind. A memory, a thought, a belief, a behavior.

4. With a deep and steady breath, release a balloon. Watch it drift away into the blue sky. It disappears, gone forever.

5. Repeat until you've let go of all your balloons.

Beginning to Loosen My Grip

Control is often rooted in fear and anxiety. You may try to control things (your feelings, your thoughts, or other people's behaviors) because it is too terrifying to think about what would happen if you didn't. Make a list of at least five fears related to relationships. How are you exerting control to calm your fears and anxieties? What are you losing when you try to control? Write about it here.

Example:

Fear: I was "too much" for my ex. I'm likely "too much" for any future partners, too. I fear I will be alone forever.

Tried to control the fear by: Taking up less emotional space, having fewer needs, and going with the flow.

What I lost: The ability to speak my mind, make requests, or enjoy small pleasures in life.

1. _____

   _____

   _____

   _____

   _____

   _____

2. _____

   _____

   _____

   _____

   _____

3. _____

_____

_____

_____

_____

_____

_____

4. _____

_____

_____

_____

_____

_____

5. _____

_____

_____

_____

_____

_____

BRINGING IT BACK TO THIS MOMENT

If you are present in this moment, you can release your anxiety and fears about future unknowns.

Create five affirmations you can use when you notice you are living in the future. After you've written them down, close your eyes, take a deep breath, and repeat each individual affirmation. Notice how your body feels as you repeat each phrase. Repeat these affirmations daily as you continue to practice letting go, releasing control, and embracing the unknown.

Example: Things will unfold as they are intended to. I can handle the unknowns in life.

1. _____
   _____
   _____
   _____

2. _____
   _____
   _____
   _____

3. _____
   _____
   _____
   _____

4. _____

_____

_____

_____

5. _____

_____

_____

_____

"What a lovely surprise to finally discover
how unlonely being alone can be."

—ELLEN BURSTYN

Making Alone Time Less Scary

When you spend time alone with yourself, you create an opportunity to better understand and connect to your feelings. If you haven't started spending more time alone since the breakup, now is the time to set the intention to do just that.

Write about any resistance you have to spending more time alone. Are you fearful that certain thoughts, memories, or feelings will creep in while you're alone? Explore ways to be alone with yourself daily. Identify three potential rituals that could make alone time feel more inviting.

Example: I'm worried I'll have spiraling thoughts if I'm alone. I can make this time more tolerable by burning candles or playing music.

1. _____
   _____
   _____
   _____

2. _____
   _____
   _____
   _____

3. _____
   _____
   _____
   _____

Alone but Not Lonely

Being alone (a physical state) and feeling lonely (an emotional state) are very separate experiences, and it is important to untangle them from one another. Can you imagine being alone without feeling lonely? What can you offer yourself during alone time to help you face any loneliness that might arise? How can you reassure yourself that loneliness after the end of a relationship is natural? Write about it here.

_____

_____

_____

_____

_____

_____

_____

_____

_____

_____

_____

_____

_____

_____

_____

Getting to Know the Real Me

What do you *hope* to learn about yourself as you begin to increase your uninterrupted time with yourself? What do you *need* to learn about yourself to continue to heal?

_____

_____

_____

_____

_____

_____

_____

_____

_____

_____

_____

_____

_____

_____

_____

_____

Allow Me to Introduce You to My Date

Plan a date with yourself. The purpose of this date is to get to know yourself better and to find your growth edge. As you plan your date, remember these guidelines:

▶ No one else is invited and there is no technology allowed on your date.

▶ Pick a date and time to take yourself out. The more specific you can be in your planning, the more likely you are to follow through.

▶ Consider places or adventures that you've always wanted to try but never have.

  Brainstorm and ultimately plan your date here.

_____

_____

_____

_____

_____

_____

_____

_____

_____

_____

_____

A Closer Look: When We Go against Our Better Judgment

I had been working with recently single Juliet for six months. She was frustrated with her perceived lack of progress, making assumptions about "how far along she should be" in her healing at this point. Juliet reported feeling "stuck," unable to find any relief from her depression. She continued to text, enable, or sleep with her ex, Riaan. Juliet would say, "I know this isn't good for me, but I can't help myself. It makes me feel bad to talk to him, and terrible not to."

Juliet felt confused: She had truly forgiven her abusive ex for the way he had treated her and the pain he inflicted. So why didn't she feel any better? Then Juliet had a breakthrough. She shared that she had cheated on Riaan two years ago. She didn't tell me because it "didn't seem important" to her, claiming she and Riaan worked through that betrayal as a couple years ago.

But Juliet hadn't worked through the betrayal with herself. She had yet to forgive *herself* for the choices she made in that relationship. She began to understand that her continued rescuing, enabling, texting, and hookups were coming from a place of guilt and repentance. As she watched Riaan struggle to grieve the end of the relationship, she began to believe she was a selfish, undeserving person for cheating on him and being a source of his pain. She lived by an unfair and untrue belief: that if she could spare him a moment of pain by answering his calls or meeting up when asked, then maybe it meant she "wasn't so awful after all." As Juliet began to forgive herself for cheating on Riaan, she took fewer of his calls. The hookups stopped entirely. She held amazing boundaries and released control. Only after forgiving herself could she truly heal.

I'd Like a Do-Over, Please

Make a list of behaviors or choices you made that you know weren't coming from the best in you. Explore and write about how you may begin to forgive yourself for these behaviors.

IDENTIFYING, CONCEPTUALIZING, AND INVITING FORGIVENESS

Quiet your surroundings and limit your distractions so you may better connect to your inner experience.

1. Ask yourself, "What does forgiveness *feel* like?" Notice what comes to mind when you ask yourself that question. Is it forgiveness of the self or of others?

2. Picture forgiveness in your body. Maybe it has a shape, texture, or color.

3. Try to conjure feelings of forgiveness. Be with that sensation for five minutes.

4. If your mind starts to wander, gently shift your focus back to your body and connect with the sensation of forgiveness.

Do I Need to Come Clean?

Earlier, you identified behaviors that hindered your healing process (see "Well, Since You Asked . . ." on page 64). Make an honest reflection. Did you hold up your end of the bargain? Recommit to the boundaries that need to be reinforced. Write about why it has been difficult to hold boundaries with yourself.

_____

_____

_____

_____

_____

_____

_____

_____

_____

_____

_____

_____

_____

_____

_____

RELEASING HOPELESSNESS TO MAKE ROOM FOR POSSIBILITIES

For this exercise, grab a blank piece of paper, scissors, a pen, matches, and a fire-safe container (perhaps a cooking pot, terra-cotta pot, or fire pit).

Cut your paper into 5 to 10 strips. On separate strips of paper, write down your unhelpful and untrue beliefs about future relationships (see "Beginning to Loosen My Grip" on page 90). As you set fire to each of these beliefs, release them from yourself. With each release, say, "I don't know yet what my future holds. I trust I will find what I need. I have the tools to take care of myself."

(If you don't jibe with those departing words, that's okay! Write your own words here to help you release control over the unknown.)

_____

_____

_____

_____

_____

_____

_____

_____

_____

Grieving What Has Yet to Come

The grieving process includes more than healing from your past experiences. You also need to grieve the losses of your future. This helps you heal as you accept the finality of the relationship. The future plans, desires, hopes, dreams, and expectations you shared with your partner are also part of the loss you're experiencing. Identify five future losses and name the emotion that accompanies each.

1. _____

_____

_____

_____

_____

_____

_____

2. _____

_____

_____

_____

_____

_____

_____

3. _____

_____

4. _____

_____

_____

_____

_____

_____

_____

_____

5. _____

_____

_____

_____

_____

_____

_____

Preventing the Dreaded Backslide

I had to face it: The Breakup was infiltrating my social, academic, and professional lives.

I ignored boundaries for myself, especially regarding not contacting my ex. My therapist helped me devise a plan to go no contact, and I began to hold myself accountable.

I started going as "no contact" as a person could possibly go on my tiny college campus. I proudly reported a few weeks, then a month, of impressive avoidance, making no contact whatsoever. I used my awareness of his whereabouts to my benefit, strategically planning my meals, extracurriculars, and social life in order to avoid him.

But then I got a little cocky. I thought I could handle seeing him, spending time around him among our mutual friends, or running into him unexpectedly. Frankly, I eventually grew tired (and a bit resentful) of planning *every little thing* around not seeing him. Out of annoyance and exhaustion, I asked my therapist, "Hey. I can do this, right? I am eating more, sleeping better, crying less. Right? I don't need to keep bending over backward to avoid him."

My therapist looked at my post-breakup shell of a self with kindness and compassion. He said, "Lindsey, you and I are studying for a test. We're gathering information, committing it to memory, and putting it into practice. This is a big test. It's not time to take the test yet."

It's easy to think we're ready to re-engage with our ex before we're *actually* ready. There can be major backslides to your healing if you take the test too early. When you start to consider possibilities of communication, in-person hangouts, or even reconciliation, it is crucial to level with yourself. Are you ready to take the test?

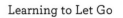

A Little Reminder

Make a list of all of the reasons you could never date your ex again. Reference this list when you're thinking about reaching out, when your mind is only focusing on the good parts of the relationship, or when you don't trust yourself to make healthy decisions regarding your ex.

_____

_____

_____

_____

_____

_____

_____

_____

_____

_____

_____

_____

_____

_____

_____

_____

What Do I Actually Miss about Those Times?

Sometimes you may think you miss your ex-partner, but really, you're missing the comfort, company, and intimacy of a relationship.

Reflect on this sentiment. Does it ring true? What do you really miss? Write about how this is or isn't true for you right now. Before you consider a possible reconciliation with your ex, it's vital to understand what's driving you.

_____

_____

_____

_____

_____

_____

_____

_____

_____

_____

_____

_____

_____

_____

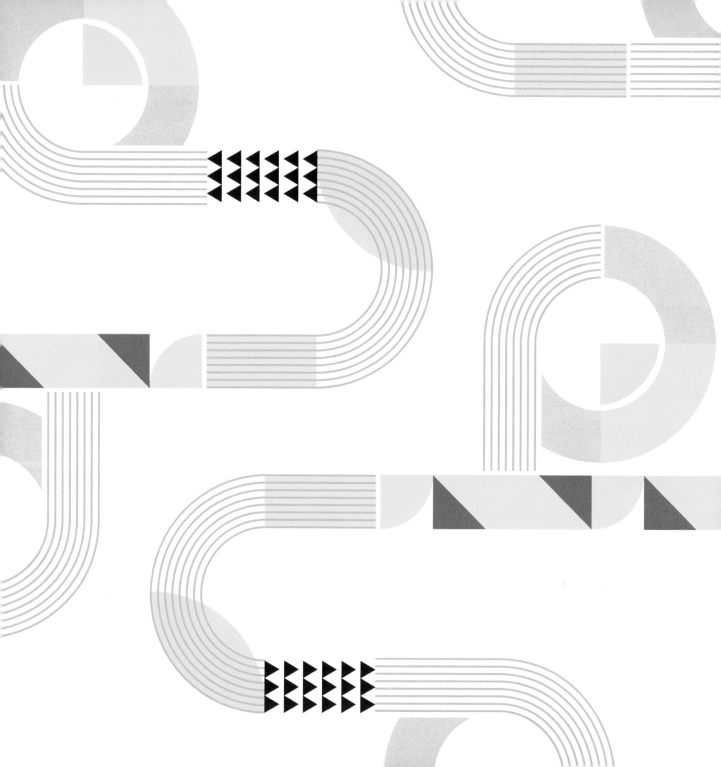

REPLENISHING YOUR SELF-WORTH

Now let's focus on bolstering your appreciation, acceptance, and sense of self. A healthy dose of self-worth paired with love and compassion toward yourself will grow your resiliency, preparing you for whatever relationships or rejections lay ahead. Consider yourself warned—this section is going to be tough! I'm not asking you to believe everything you write, but I am asking you to *practice* believing it. Many prompts are designed for you to reread daily to set the foundation for a new relationship with yourself and others. As you begin to *actually integrate* practices of self-love, you'll notice that everything changes.

"What lies behind us and what lies before us are tiny matters compared to what lies within us."

—RALPH WALDO EMERSON

Honoring Your Truth vs. Honoring Your Anxiety

Jordan wanted to understand why she couldn't get a relationship off the ground. She had no trouble initiating a date or approaching someone who caught her eye. But she always had seemingly rational reasons to call it off after the first date. Soon I realized that anxiety, not incompatibility, was the real culprit.

Jordan wanted to listen to that voice inside that warned her of red flags. When that voice said he wasn't a good match or wouldn't be able to meet her needs, Jordan blindly listened in the name of "honoring her truth." But she was actually honoring her anxiety.

Anxiety can be informative. It can keep us safe and warn us of a threat. But sometimes the anxiety we feel has nothing to do with what's going on in that moment. When we teach ourselves to discern between the two, we learn to trust ourselves.

Typically, Jordan would inform her date she wasn't interested *while she was still on the date.* Her friends reinforced this behavior, calling her fiercely independent and "not willing to settle." As she practiced learning to trust herself, Jordan began to slow down this process. She began ending dates by saying, "I'll follow up with you sometime this week and let you know how I'm feeling." Then, she waited.

She still felt anxiety after every date, but now she waited it out. Some anxiety faded overnight. This usually indicated her body wasn't warning her of red flags. Some anxiety stayed for days. In these cases, she stayed curious and usually determined there was something actually "off." Through her curiosity and slowing down, she was able to listen to herself differently, ultimately leading her on many great second dates.

Whose Scripts Am I Following, Anyway?

The thoughts in your head aren't always your own. They may be scripts and stories others have handed to you. Maybe the belief that you "aren't good enough" is a parental voice from childhood. Perhaps the idea that you're "too much" is the voice of your ex.

Write down five thoughts you've had about yourself lately. Whose words are they? It is vital to follow the scripts about your worth that the *healthiest version of yourself* has written. Ditch the other scripts.

1. _____
_____
_____
_____
_____
_____
_____

2. _____
_____
_____
_____
_____
_____
_____

3. _____
   _____
   _____
   _____
   _____
   _____
   _____

4. _____
   _____
   _____
   _____
   _____
   _____
   _____

5. _____
   _____
   _____
   _____
   _____
   _____
   _____

Befriending My Inner Critic

Write a letter to your inner critic (that inner voice that's been relentlessly judging you for past thoughts, behaviors, and feelings). Don't tell the voice to go away, as that usually makes it get louder! Instead, be curious about where it came from and why it's adamant about bringing you down. Befriend this voice so it's a bit less intimidating.

_____

_____

_____

_____

_____

_____

_____

_____

_____

_____

_____

_____

_____

_____

_____

_____

How Did I Learn to Treat Myself This Way?

When do you find it hardest to love yourself? Reflect on how you learned to relate to yourself in this way.

Example: I am especially hard on myself when I'm not productive enough, am lonely, or after I've made a mistake.

_____

_____

_____

_____

_____

_____

_____

_____

_____

_____

_____

_____

_____

_____

_____

Respect Your Fear of Spiders, Not Your Fear of Dating

Write down five fears you have about starting to date again. Address your fears as if you were talking to a friend. Validate your feelings but challenge their reality.

Example: I'm afraid I'll never find someone who can accept my flaws. → *It's true, I have flaws. That doesn't make me undatable. People are imperfect and find love every day.*

1. _____

_____

_____

_____

_____

_____

_____

2. _____

_____

_____

_____

_____

_____

_____

3. _____

_____

_____

_____

_____

_____

_____

4. _____

_____

_____

_____

_____

_____

_____

5. _____

_____

_____

_____

_____

_____

_____

LEARNING TO TRUST YOURSELF AGAIN

Throughout this breakup journey, you've been developing your sense of "knowing" yourself—who you truly are underneath your history, heartbreak, and reactivity. This has all been a part of you learning to trust yourself again. When you trust yourself, you can hold better boundaries, ask for what you want and need, speak up, and inherently know your worth. One way you can build trust in yourself is to continuously show up for you! When you make a commitment to yourself and then follow through, you further establish and grow trust in yourself.

Make a daily promise to yourself. It could be anything! Do you want to drink 60 ounces of water every day? Maybe you want to commit to eating breakfast daily or sleep with no electronics in your room. Make a promise to yourself and stick to it for a week. Notice how it feels to keep promises to yourself. If you break a promise, extend compassion and patience to yourself and start again tomorrow.

Normalizing and Welcoming Praise

It's hard to accept the "unpolished" parts of yourself, but it can also be hard to accept praise or recognition from yourself or others. Make a list of 10 compliments you can give yourself. Bookmark this page to read your list every day.

1. _____

2. _____

3. _____

4. _____

5. _____

6. _____

7. _____

8. _____

9. _____

10. _____

BOUNDARY SETTING: A LIFELONG PRACTICE (HOPEFULLY!)

Repetition is essential if you want to shift your thought and behavioral patterns, and when it comes to learning to trust yourself, there's no such thing as too much practice. After all, you already hold all the answers for healing within yourself (no, really!). But you must learn to listen and *trust* your healthiest inner voice.

Boundaries play a vital role in building trust. It's a powerful practice to set boundaries on your time, energy, and space. When you set a boundary, you're signaling that you know *you are worthy of respect. You* **are** *worthy of respect, so it's important to act that way!*

Remember, a boundary is simply something you are/are not okay with. Set one boundary today (it can be small, like not taking a call when you don't have the emotional bandwidth, or declining an invite for after-work drinks because you have a date with a book). Notice how it feels after you hold your boundary. You may feel nervous or timid, like you did something wrong. Just breathe through it. Maybe you'll feel empowered and brave. Just notice. Regardless of how you feel, know that it's always okay to take care of yourself.

Self-Love As a Practice, Not a Construct

How does a person worthy of love treat themselves? Include three behaviors and three boundaries in your reflection.

Behaviors

1. _____

_____

_____

_____

_____

2. _____

_____

_____

_____

_____

3. _____

_____

_____

_____

_____

Boundaries

1. _____

   _____

   _____

   _____

   _____

   _____

2. _____

   _____

   _____

   _____

   _____

   _____

3. _____

   _____

   _____

   _____

   _____

   _____

Calling Out Future Excuses

What are reasons you may start to date again, even if you don't feel emotionally ready? Have you ever started a relationship before you were ready? What stories might you tell yourself to convince yourself you're ready when you really aren't?

_____

_____

_____

_____

_____

_____

_____

_____

_____

_____

_____

_____

_____

_____

_____

_____

_____

CREATING EXTERNAL CUES FOR INTERNAL PROCESSING

It requires intention and practice to build self-love, worth, and compassion. Early attempts to build these tenets can feel unnatural, fake, or just plain stupid. Consider this: Pretend you've decided to write a letter with your nondominant hand. You'd naturally and automatically use your dominant hand to pick up the pen. You might then laugh, switch hands, and produce a terribly messy or illegible letter. You'd expect that because it's new. You'd expect to be bad at it. You'd give yourself grace, and you'd keep trying.

When it comes to loving or accepting yourself, don't expect yourself to "just get it." But with an intentional practice and commitment to honing these skills, it can soon become a lot easier to pick up the pen with the proverbial nondominant hand.

What words, affirmations, or reminders do you need to see daily so you can begin to integrate them into your life more easily? Maybe "It's okay to be imperfect," "Healing isn't linear," or that you want to take a walk after dinner. Write them on sticky notes and place them around the house. These reminders will help you relate to yourself differently, creating lasting change.

There Are Worse Things Than Being Single

What have you loved about being single? When have you experienced joy since the breakup? It's important to remember that being single ≠ undesirable, bad, or something you need to change.

_____

_____

_____

_____

_____

_____

_____

_____

_____

_____

_____

_____

_____

_____

_____

_____

When You're Always Drinking and Always Thirsty

You're terribly thirsty, and you've found a well. But you only have a slotted spoon. You try to bring water to your mouth with the spoon. With enough urgency and repetition, you get enough drops to stave off dehydration, but you keep going back for more. It's never enough. You are never quite satisfied, surviving but always thirsty.

This is what it can feel like to place our worthiness in someone else's hands. We feel thirsty for more when we rely on others for validation, happiness, or steadiness in our life. If we use others' opinions, needs, demands, expectations, or feedback as our sole sense of nourishment, we will never be satisfied. We have to get those things from ourselves.

Stay curious about ways you might be drinking with a slotted spoon, placing your worthiness in the hands of others.

Shifting Your Source of Validation

It's difficult to stop relying on others for validation, but crucial to source it from ourselves. The shift doesn't come easy, so start by building on what you already have. Make a list of five things you enjoy or are good at. Brainstorm a way to expand upon your already existing talent (then do it!). Remember: Any action or plan you include needs to be for *you* and no one else.

Example: I enjoy running.

I will sign up for a 10k.

I make the best rhubarb crumble.

I'll make some and share with coworkers or neighbors, just because.

It's Okay to Brag on Myself

What friend or family member knows you best? Imagine asking them, "Why do you feel lucky to have me in your life?" Really try to capture their perspective. Notice what feels easy to believe and what feels difficult to accept. Write their answers and reflect on them here.

_____

_____

_____

_____

_____

_____

_____

"When you recover or discover something that nourishes your soul and brings joy, care enough about yourself to make room for it in your life."

—JEAN SHINDODA BOLEN

WHEN THE LITTLE THINGS IN LIFE ARE ACTUALLY THE BIG THINGS

One day my daughter was laughing and squealing as she jumped in a mud puddle on our afternoon hike. I humored her for about 10 seconds, then said, "Okay, let's go!" She looked at me like I was crazy, as if to ask, "Why would we ever stop having this much fun?" She had a good point. I took a deep breath, released my agenda for the next 10 minutes, and joined her. I mean, really joined her. I got my clothes muddy, I was late to meet a friend, and I had the biggest smile on my face. Before my daughter stopped our walk to jump, I was thinking about the moments ahead: what's for dinner, what route I'll take to meet my friend, how much longer our walk would take. She brought me back to that moment in time. I felt free.

Set an intention to play today. Look for opportunities to find joy, be silly, or take the scenic route. Notice what it feels like to connect to those "kid" parts of you again. Healing isn't just confronting the past and deep thinking. It also looks like choosing joy, playing, or even jumping in mud puddles.

Are You a Leaf Pile Jumper or a Belly Laugher?

One way you can develop self-love is through play! Many adults leave the "playing" for kids, but a 2013 study published in the *European Journal of Humour Research* shows it is equally important for adult mental wellness. It can improve your mood, relieve stress, and create connection with yourself and others. Reflect on the way you relate to playing, and the role it has in your life. How do you feel when you play?

_____

_____

_____

_____

_____

_____

_____

_____

_____

_____

_____

_____

_____

Changing What I Can, Accepting What I Can't

What are five things about yourself that impact your confidence? Write them here. Which ones can you change? Which ones do you need to accept? Changing what you can and accepting what you can't is an important step in your healing journey. Leave your appearance out of this discussion—your body is the least exciting thing about you!

Example: I don't know how to talk to new people, and it keeps me quiet and shut down in groups. → This is a learned skill that I can practice. That will help build my confidence.

1. _____

_____

2. _____

_____

3. _____

_____

4. _____

_____

5. _____

_____

UNDERSTANDING WHEN I'M READY TO DATE

Can't tell if you're actually ready to date or if you're just over being alone? Maybe this can help you sort it out. Only you can know when you're really ready. Add to the list based on what you know about yourself.

DATING TO AVOID BEING ALONE	DATING BECAUSE I'M READY
Things are moving really quickly with a new partner.	*I have structure in my life. I don't neglect structure or routine when I am attracted to a new person.*
There are red flags I am unwilling to see or am quick to ignore.	*I am willing to take things slow.*
I am not aware of "how I'm doing" or what I'm feeling outside of this new attraction.	*I know what I want in a relationship.*
Time alone is still unbearable.	*I am managing my alone time and look forward to it.*
I am intolerant of being bored.	*I value my independence.*
I focus on what others want or what would make them happy.	*I have turned down interested parties that didn't seem like a good match. I won't settle.*

Healthy Expectations for Healthy Relationships

You can't be everything for one person, and one person can't be everything for you. Much like you leaned on different people after the breakup, you need to lean on a variety of people while you are partnered, too. What has your experience taught you to expect from a future partner? What are the liabilities with these roles? What roles can be better filled by more secure, consistent figures in your life?

_____

_____

_____

_____

_____

_____

_____

_____

_____

_____

_____

_____

_____

_____

_____

_____

Nothing Is Personal

Research shows that breakups are harder to process for individuals who personalize rejection. How would your life be different if you took nothing personally? Imagine what dating would look like if you took nothing personally. Write about it here.

_____

_____

_____

_____

_____

_____

_____

_____

_____

_____

_____

_____

_____

_____

_____

_____

Am I Being Fair to Myself?

How are your beliefs about yourself holding you back from meeting new people? What beliefs do you need to relinquish?

_____

_____

_____

_____

_____

_____

_____

_____

_____

_____

_____

_____

_____

_____

_____

_____

GETTING BACK OUT THERE

In this section you'll come to understand that rejection is a part of life, nothing is personal, and that it's always worth it to be honest with yourself and a potential partner. The following prompts and exercises will guide you in practices of vulnerability and honesty to help pave the way for authentic, compatible, and healthy partnership. I'll challenge you to leave old dating habits in the past and to adopt new ones. It may not be easy, *but* I'm confident these strategies will lead you to more fulfilling partnerships.

Honing My Gut Instinct

Imagine a time when you *knew* something was off in your relationship. Maybe your body was telling you a partner was being dishonest or that something felt wrong. What did that feel like in your body? If you can't remember what it felt like, *imagine* what it felt like when your body was trying to give you information.

_____

_____

_____

_____

_____

_____

_____

_____

_____

_____

_____

_____

_____

_____

_____

_____

WHEN BEING SINGLE ISN'T A REFLECTION ON YOUR WORTH

Write out five statements that finish this sentence:

I can be single and still be _____.

1. _____
   _____
   _____
   _____
   _____

2. _____
   _____
   _____
   _____
   _____

3. _____
   _____
   _____
   _____
   _____

4. _____

_____

_____

_____

_____

5. _____

_____

_____

_____

_____

Reread your statements. Take a deep breath. Starting at the top of your head and ending at your feet, track how each body part feels after reading these statements. Refer back to this exercise when you need to remind yourself that being single isn't a character flaw.

Learning to Date with Intention and Integrity

Gabriella was exhausted by the dating scene. She was constantly disappointed by her options of available men and frequently threatened to give up on dating altogether. She was tired of being let down after she'd go on a date, only to learn mid-date that she had nothing in common with these prospective partners.

As I watched Gabriella feel stuck in this cycle of horrible dates, I began to ask her about the dates themselves. How was she meeting prospective partners? What would they do together when they met in person?

Gabriella told me that she met most of her dates on a dating app, quickly stating, "I hate dating apps. I don't even know why I'm on there." She then expressed hope in meeting someone at a local bar. I was familiar with the bar and their house band, and I mentioned that I didn't realize she enjoyed punk rock music. She quickly replied, "That's because I don't! I can't stand it. I just go there because my roommate's partner works there." Gabriella further explained how she'd much rather be in her bed by 9:00 p.m. reading a book.

Why would Gabriella think she would find a compatible partner through an app she resents, at a bar that she doesn't enjoy, and at a time of night that she'd rather be someplace else? Gabriella was on the apps because she "figured she had to be" and at the bar because she followed her friend there. Neither of those choices were aligned with her values or priorities (in-person connection, rest, and alone time, to name a few). Gabriella adjusted her dating approach and began to spend more time creating connections at the dog park and her local coffee shop. She even joined a club volleyball team and a book club. Suddenly, she understood she had many dating options after all, but she had been looking in the wrong place.

Understanding My Values

Personal values are standards you adopt that represent what is important to you in life. Make a list of your top five personal values. If you need help, reference a list of core values you can find with a quick Google search. These are values that *you* want to live by.

For each value, write an example of what it looks like to live by that value. When you lead with your values, your decisions are more likely to lead you to prolonged satisfaction or happiness.

Example: I value curiosity. Applied, this looks like leading with curiosity instead of judgment when I don't understand someone's behavior.

1. _____
_____
_____
_____
_____

2. _____
_____
_____
_____
_____

3. _____
_____
_____

4. _____

_____

_____

_____

_____

5. _____

_____

_____

_____

_____

When it comes to dating, you probably feel out of practice. That's because you are out of practice! But there's good news: Being authentic doesn't go out of style.

Unpacking Intentionality

What does the phrase "dating intentionally" mean to you?

_____

What are five ways *you* can date intentionally when you're ready?

1. _____

   _____

2. _____

   _____

3. _____

   _____

4. _____

   _____

5. _____

   _____

It's Okay to Have Nonnegotiables

What are your nonnegotiables for a partner? Focus more on qualities instead of behaviors. Bring attention to what you *do* want from them versus what you don't want.

Example: "My future partner must be able to hear feedback," vs. "My future partner won't get defensive and mad."

_____

_____

_____

_____

_____

_____

_____

_____

_____

_____

_____

_____

_____

_____

_____

_____

Good News—There Are Steps to Follow

Dr. John Van Epp created the Relationship Attachment Model (RAM) to educate singles on how to engage in a healthy relationship progression. His research shows the importance of developing these dynamics in a very specific order: Know, Trust, Rely, Commit, and Touch. That is, in healthy relationships you *know* someone more than you *trust* them, *trust* someone more than you *rely* on them, *rely* on them more than you *commit,* and are more *committed* than you are physically intimate (*touch*). When you don't follow this progression, you often end up getting hurt and disappointed.

   Have you followed this progression in the past? Briefly write about which order you followed in your last relationship.

_____

_____

_____

_____

_____

_____

_____

_____

_____

_____

_____

_____

_____

Putting It into Practice

Outline specific actions that follow the progression of Know, Trust, Rely, Commit, and Touch. What does it look like in practice for you to follow these steps? Be as specific as possible.

_____

_____

_____

_____

_____

_____

_____

_____

_____

_____

_____

_____

_____

_____

_____

_____

Green, Yellow, and Red Relationship Flags

You've heard of relationship red flags, but have you considered green or yellow flags? Like a traffic light, each color indicates an action: Green for "go," yellow for "slow down," and red for "stop." Make a list of at least five examples for each category. Focus on *patterns* instead of singular events or preferences (such as appearance or career).

GREEN FLAGS	YELLOW FLAGS	RED FLAGS

When Waiting Is Worth It

Three months after The Breakup, I was excited for a change of scenery, anticipating my summer job at a camp on the Appalachian Trail. I reconnected with another staff member named Phillip via texts and calls. We were both newly single, extremely heartbroken, and really into each other. Neither of us was honest about our post-breakup mental health. It just felt good to be connected to someone else and not think about our exes.

But there was no denying my depression or my attempts to hide from it. I couldn't pretend that I was "over it" or had healed from my breakup trauma. But I knew two things to be true: that I wasn't ready to date, and that I wanted to date Phillip anyway.

Despite my better judgment, I told Phillip I wanted to date him as we parted ways at the end of the summer. He took an intentional week to confront his own healing and sort out his wants from his needs. He said it wasn't the right time and that he needed to grow and heal more (and suspected I did, too). I felt disappointed and rejected. We went our separate ways, me to Memphis and him to Raleigh.

Three months later, I called Phillip and told him I was visiting Raleigh and would like to see him. We had both healed a lot since we last saw each other; neither of us needed a quick fix for our sadness, and we weren't reactive to our emotions. That trip to Raleigh started a slow, intentional, sometimes bumpy, often wonderful relationship. We got married five years later. I thank Phillip often for trusting himself and his needs as he waited to pursue a relationship. A relationship's foundation is only as strong as the individuals in it. Our story would have likely ended differently (and a lot sooner) had we built our relationship on the backs of our heartbreak.

CONNECTING IN A SAFE SPACE

Make a date with a totally platonic friend. Invite them to share an activity or adventure that you enjoy. Get excited and make it intentional. Is there a cool waterfall that you'd be excited to share? Do they need to taste the best milkshake you've ever had that is two hours away?

This is not a "practice date" for your next love interest. This is an opportunity for you to intentionally share excitement and enthusiasm with a person who cares about you. It's a challenge for you to do something special, have fun, and build connection. Be open to a new kind of experience that can help you accept adventure, love, trust, and connection.

Assessing Your Expectations to Mitigate Resentment

Resentment and disappointment thrive on unrealistic expectations. Often, these expectations go unnamed to yourself, and certainly remain unnamed to a date or new partner. Make a list of five expectations you have for a first date.

1. _____
   _____
   _____
   _____

2. _____
   _____
   _____
   _____

3. _____
   _____
   _____
   _____

4. _____
   _____
   _____
   _____

5. _____

_____

_____

_____

Reflect on your list of expectations. Which expectations are you willing to communicate on or before a first date? Are these expectations realistic? Are they within your realm of control? Reflect here.

Example: Unrealistic expectations include "I will just know if this person is a right fit for me after our first date. I should be able to feel it." Or, the expectation that your date will willingly pick up the tab seems unfair, especially without communication involved.

_____

_____

_____

_____

_____

_____

_____

_____

_____

_____

_____

Communicating Differently

What does healthy communication look like in a relationship? How do you need to communicate differently in your next relationship? How might different communication provide clarity for you as you choose a partner?

_____

_____

_____

_____

_____

_____

_____

_____

_____

_____

_____

_____

_____

_____

_____

_____

CONFIDENCE BEFORE COURAGE

When my clients say they want more confidence, they actually mean they want more courage. Set a goal to do something courageous today. This should be a low-stakes risk, like sitting alone at a coffee shop, finally trying out your new rollerblades in public, or wearing that new outfit that feels a little intimidating. Notice what it feels like in your body to take a risk. Notice how you feel in your body when you do the hard, courageous thing. Take it a step further to make this a daily practice. Courage comes before confidence, and repetition creates it.

Unpacking Unhelpful Rules I've Made for Myself

Decisions are often rooted in unhelpful, untrue, or unfair beliefs. Sometimes, you don't even realize you hold a specific belief, let alone realize it is driving your decisions. What beliefs do you have as they relate to dating again? Write five examples using this format: I must feel _____ before I can _____. Then, challenge this belief. Remember, specific feelings are not a prerequisite to action.

Example: "I must feel confident before I can date." This is false. It would be easier, smoother, and less risky to date if I felt confident, but by no means is confidence a requirement to start dating again.

1. _____

_____

_____

_____

_____

_____

2. _____

_____

_____

_____

_____

_____

3. _____

_____

_____

_____

_____

_____

4. _____

_____

_____

_____

_____

_____

5. _____

_____

_____

_____

_____

_____

When Rejection Is Just a Part of Life

Most people are rejection avoidant after a breakup, so it is likely that you will avoid (perceived) risks, leaving you less likely to meet new people or open up to others out of fear of being hurt. Normalizing and depersonalizing rejection can help dating again seem less intimidating.

Name five people who you enjoy spending time with but would never want to date.

6. _____

7. _____

8. _____

9. _____

10. _____

Write about how this is not a rejection of these people. Practice not making rejection personal.

_____

_____

_____

_____

_____

_____

_____

GETTING OUTSIDE MY COMFORT ZONE

Today, strike up a conversation with someone you normally wouldn't. Maybe it's the barista, someone at the bus stop, or the person who is sharing your elevator. Don't just say, "Hi, how are you?" Ask them something personal, yet appropriate ("I love your glasses! Where did you get them? How was your experience there?") or share a feeling with them ("I always feel so happy when I walk into your shop. It's so inviting and warm."). Be authentically you. Authentically connecting to folks in your world will enrich your life. Not to mention, it can help you get over those fears of dating again.

That Time I Got It Wrong

As it relates to dating, write about a time that you got it wrong and things weren't as they seemed. Maybe you incorrectly assumed someone wasn't interested in you or that a partner was lying when they weren't. Name the emotions and thoughts that led you to an untrue assumption. What can you learn from this experience?

_____

_____

_____

_____

_____

_____

_____

_____

_____

_____

_____

_____

_____

_____

_____

_____

Dating Differently

So many folks ask a potential partner to coffee or to grab a drink for a first date. As you reenter the dating world, consider doing this differently. Coffee dates yield very little information about a person, and they operate more like an interview.

Make a list of six ideas for a different kind of date. What kind of experiences would you enjoy sharing with someone else and why? What can you learn about a person by observing them in these scenarios?

1. _____
   _____
   _____
   _____
   _____
   _____

2. _____
   _____
   _____
   _____
   _____

3. _____
   _____
   _____

4. _____

_____

_____

_____

_____

5. _____

_____

_____

_____

_____

6. _____

_____

_____

_____

_____

I CAN HANDLE THE MOMENT
IN FRONT OF ME

You're anticipating the first date since the breakup. Or maybe it's the first intentional, non-rebound date. You're excited. Set the intention to be present as you get ready for your date. As you get ready continuously bring your attention back to that moment.

It's really easy to start living in the future when we feel nervous or anxious. Unfortunately, this only adds to our anxiety. It is not uncommon to wonder in anticipation of a date: "Will they like me?" "What if I'm about to meet my person?" "What if this is the last first date I ever go on?" Maybe your internal dialogue is more pessimistic, like "I know this will be a bust," "This is a waste of time," or other assumptions about your date's character, personality, or interests.

As you learn to honor your own inner voice, you'll also learn to appreciate when others do the same. You'll appreciate when they're honest with themselves and with you, even if it's hard to hear what they're saying. This is what it looks like when honoring yourself is more important than having a partner.

But Do They Deserve You?

Your job is not to worry about whether you're a good match for your new love interest. Your job is to determine whether they are a good match for *you*. Don't get it backward. Name three emotions or sensations you feel in your body when you reread that truth. What visual comes to mind that represents this sentiment? Write about it here.

_____

_____

_____

_____

_____

_____

_____

_____

_____

_____

_____

Review your answer and imagine this visual as you prepare for a first date.

RESOURCES

Websites

OpenPathCollective.org

TheBreakupTherapist.com

InclusiveTherapists.com

Books

Attached: The New Science of Adult Attachment and How It Can Help You Find—and Keep—Love, by Amir Levine and Rachel S. F. Heller

Polysecure: Attachment, Trauma and Consensual Nonmonogamy, by Jessica Fern

Set Boundaries, Find Peace: A Guide to Reclaiming Yourself, by Nedra Glover Tawwab

Maybe You Should Talk to Someone, by Lori Gottlieb

Group: How One Therapist and a Group of Strangers Saved My Life, by Christie Tate

Conscious Uncoupling: 5 Steps to Living Happily Ever *After,* by Katherine Woodward Thomas

Podcasts

Where Should We Begin? with Esther Perel

The Hidden Brain with Shankar Vedantam

Apps

Headspace: Meditation & Sleep

REFERENCES

André, Christophe. "Proper Breathing Brings Better Health." *Scientific American*. January 15, 2019. www.scientificamerican.com/article/proper-breathing-brings-better-health.

Becker-Phelps, Leslie. "Don't Just React: Choose Your Response." *Psychology Today*. July 23, 2013. www.psychologytoday.com/us/blog/making-change/201307/dont-just -react-choose-your-response.

Bolen, Jean Shinoda. *Crones Don't Whine: Concentrated Wisdom for Juicy Women*. Ireland: Mango Media, 2003.

Burns, David D. *The Feeling Good Handbook*. New York: Plume, 2020.

Carlyle, Thomas. *On Heroes, Hero-Worship, And The Heroic In History*. London: Oxford University Press 1966.

Coelho, Paulo. *The Alchemist: A Fable About Following Your Dream*. London: HarperCollins, 2006.

Gascoine, Jim. "CMN Podcast Episode 16: Relationship Attachment Model (RAM)." *Codependency No More* podcast. June 22, 2015. www.codependencynomore.com /session16.

Heid, Markham. "You Asked: Can a Breakup Make You Sick?" *Time*. September 20, 2017. time.com/4949554/how-to-get-over-a-break-up.

Howe, Lauren. "A Psychologist Explains Why Some People Take Breakups Harder Than Others." *The Atlantic*. January 20, 2016. www.theatlantic.com/health/archive/2016/01 /romantic-rejection-and-the-self-deprecation-trap/424842.

Julson, Erica. "10 Best Ways to Increase Dopamine Levels Naturally." Healthline. May 10, 2018. www.healthline.com/nutrition/how-to-increase-dopamine.

Richards, Stephen. *How To Get Everything You Can Imagine: Volume 1*. Tyneside, UK: Mirage Media, 2014.

Previte, Ashley. "*Stretch Your Body, Stretch Your Mind*." Resilient Educator. Accessed May 21, 2021. resilienteducator.com/lifestyle/body-stretch-exercises.

Proyer, René T. "The Well-Being of Playful Adults: Adult Playfulness, Subjective Well-Being, Physical Well-Being, and the Pursuit of Enjoyable Activities." *European Journal of Humour Research* 1, no. 1 (March 2013): 84–98. doi:10.7592/ejhr2013.1.1.proyer.

Thomas, Katherine Woodward. *Conscious Uncoupling: 5 Steps to Living Happily* Ever *After*. New York: Harmony, 2016.

Acknowledgments

Thank you to Rob Dove, LCSW, for being a light all those years ago. In more ways than one, I wouldn't be here today without you. Thank you for helping me find my footing, teaching me how to love myself again, and setting me on this life-changing path of self-discovery. Forever grateful.

A big thank-you to my supervisor and mentor, Elizabeth Heaney, MA, LPC, for your clinical guidance on this project. Thank you for pushing me to always dig deeper and for challenging me to stay curious in both my clinical practice and personal relationships. I am a better therapist and partner because I met you.

Sincerely, words cannot describe the impact you both have had on my life.

About the Author

**Lindsey Dortch Brock, LCSW**, (she/her) never thought a breakup could be the best thing to ever happen to her. Her intro to therapy was a last-ditch effort to "get back to normal" that quickly turned into a lifelong practice of healing and self-discovery. Inspired by the role a therapist played in her life, Lindsey graduated with her MSW from the University of Pittsburgh School of Social Work with a focus in Direct Clinical Practice. Lindsey supports individuals and couples through breakups and betrayals in both her psychotherapy practice in North Carolina and international coaching practice. Lindsey is equally passionate about helping you not date jerks as she is about keeping her fiddle leaf fig alive. She lives with her husband, daughter, and pup in Asheville, North Carolina.